Great Works Instructional Guides for Literature

The GIVER

A guide for the novel by Lois Lowry
Great Works Author: Kristin Kemp

SHELL EDUCATION

Publishing Credits

Robin Erickson, *Production Director;* Lee Aucoin, *Creative Director;* Timothy J. Bradley, *Illustration Manager;* Emily R. Smith, M.A.Ed., *Editorial Director;* Amber Goff, *Editorial Assistant;* Don Tran, *Production Supervisor;* Corinne Burton, M.A.Ed., *Publisher*

Image Credits

Cover S-F/Shutterstock, Denphumi/Shutterstock, Monkey Business Images/Shutterstock

Standards

© 2007 Teachers of English to Speakers of Other Languages, Inc. (TESOL)
© 2007 Board of Regents of the University of Wisconsin System. World-Class Instructional Design and Assessment (WIDA).
© Copyright 2010. National Governors Association Center for Best Practices and Council of Chief State School Officers. All rights reserved

Shell Education

5301 Oceanus Drive
Huntington Beach, CA 92649-1030
http://www.shelleducation.com
ISBN 978-1-4258-8978-4
© 2014 Shell Educational Publishing, Inc.

Table of Contents

How to Use This Literature Guide

Today's standards demand rigor and relevance in the reading of complex texts. The units in this series guide teachers in a rich and deep exploration of worthwhile works of literature for classroom study. The most rigorous instruction can also be interesting and engaging!

Many current strategies for effective literacy instruction have been incorporated into these instructional guides for literature. Throughout the units, text-dependent questions are used to determine comprehension of the book as well as student interpretation of the vocabulary words. The books chosen for the series are complex exemplars of carefully crafted works of literature. Close reading is used throughout the units to guide students toward revisiting the text and using textual evidence to respond to prompts orally and in writing. Students must analyze the story elements in multiple assignments for each section of the book. All of these strategies work together to rigorously guide students through their study of literature.

The next few pages will make clear how to use this guide for a purposeful and meaningful literature study. Each section of this guide is set up in the same way to make it easier for you to implement the instruction in your classroom.

Theme Thoughts

The great works of literature used throughout this series have important themes that have been relevant to people for many years. Many of the themes will be discussed during the various sections of this instructional guide. However, it would also benefit students to have independent time to think about the key themes of the novel.

Before students begin reading, have them complete *Pre-Reading Theme Thoughts* (page 13). This graphic organizer will allow students to think about the themes outside the context of the story. They'll have the opportunity to evaluate statements based on important themes and defend their opinions. Be sure to have students keep their papers for comparison to the *Post-Reading Theme Thoughts* (page 64). This graphic organizer is similar to the pre-reading activity. However, this time, students will be answering the questions from the point of view of one of the characters of the novel. They have to think about how the character would feel about each statement and defend their thoughts. To conclude the activity, have students compare what they thought about the themes before the novel to what the characters discovered during the story.

How to Use This Literature Guide (cont.)

Vocabulary

Each teacher overview page has definitions and sentences about how key vocabulary words are used in the section. These words should be introduced and discussed with students. There are two student vocabulary activity pages in each section. On the first page, students are asked to define the words chosen by the author of this unit. On the second page in most sections, each student will select words that he or she finds interesting or difficult. For each section, choose one of these pages for your students to complete. With either assignment, you may want to have students get into pairs to discuss the meanings of the words. Allow students to use reference guides to define the words. Monitor students to make sure the definitions they have found are accurate and relate to how the words are used in the text.

On some of the vocabulary student pages, students are asked to answer text-related questions about the vocabulary words. The following question stems will help you create your own vocabulary questions if you'd like to extend the discussion.

- How does this word describe _____'s character?
- In what ways does this word relate to the problem in this story?
- How does this word help you understand the setting?
- In what ways is this word related to the story's solution?
- Describe how this word supports the novel's theme of _____.
- What visual images does this word bring to your mind?
- For what reasons might the author have chosen to use this particular word?

At times, more work with the words will help students understand their meanings. The following quick vocabulary activities are a good way to further study the words.

- Have students practice their vocabulary and writing skills by creating sentences and/or paragraphs in which multiple vocabulary words are used correctly and with evidence of understanding.
- Students can play vocabulary concentration. Students make a set of cards with the words and a separate set of cards with the definitions. Then, students lay the cards out on the table and play concentration. The goal of the game is to match vocabulary words with their definitions.
- Students can create word journal entries about the words. Students choose words they think are important and then describe why they think each word is important within the novel.

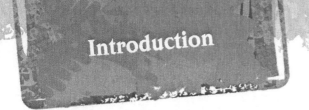

How to Use This Literature Guide *(cont.)*

Analyzing the Literature

After students have read each section, hold small-group or whole-class discussions. Questions are written at two levels of complexity to allow you to decide which questions best meet the needs of your students. The Level 1 questions are typically less abstract than the Level 2 questions. Level 1 is indicated by a square, while Level 2 is indicated by a triangle.

These questions focus on the various story elements, such as character, setting, and plot. Student pages are provided if you want to assign these questions for individual student work before your group discussion. Be sure to add further questions as your students discuss what they've read. For each question, a few key points are provided for your reference as you discuss the novel with students.

Reader Response

In today's classrooms, there are often great readers who are below average writers. So much time and energy is spent in classrooms getting students to read on grade level, that little time is left to focus on writing skills. To help teachers include more writing in their daily literacy instruction, each section of this guide has a literature-based reader response prompt. Each of the three genres of writing is used in the reader responses within this guide: narrative, informative/explanatory, and opinion/argument. Students have a choice between two prompts for each reader response. One response requires students to make connections between the reading and their own lives. The other prompt requires students to determine text-to-text connections or connections within the text.

Close Reading the Literature

Within each section, students are asked to closely reread a short section of text. Since some versions of the novels have different page numbers, the selections are described by chapter and location along with quotations to guide the readers. After each close reading, there are text-dependent questions to be answered by students.

Encourage students to read each question one at a time and then go back to the text and discover the answer. Work with students to ensure that they use the text to determine their answers rather than making unsupported inferences. Once students have answered the questions, discuss what they discovered. Suggested answers are provided in the answer key.

How to Use This Literature Guide (cont.)

Close Reading the Literature (cont.)

These generic, open-ended stems can be used to write your own text-dependent questions if you would like to give students more practice.

- Give evidence from the text to support . . . .
- Justify your thinking using text evidence about . . . .
- Find evidence to support your conclusions about . . . .
- What text evidence helps the reader understand . . . ?
- Use the book to tell why _____ happens.
- Based on events in the story, ...
- Use text evidence to tell why . . . .

Making Connections

The activities in this section help students make cross-curricular connections to writing, mathematics, science, social studies, or the fine arts. In some of these lessons, students are asked to use the author as a mentor. The writing in the novel models a skill for them that they can then try to emulate. Students may also be asked to look for examples of language conventions within the novel. Each of these types of activities requires higher-order thinking skills from students.

Creating with the Story Elements

It is important to spend time discussing the common story elements in literature. Understanding the characters, setting, and plot can increase students' comprehension and appreciation of the story. If teachers discuss these elements daily, students will more likely internalize the concepts and look for the elements in their independent reading. Another important reason for focusing on the story elements is that students will be better writers if they think about how the stories they read are constructed.

Students are given three options for working with the story elements. They are asked to create something related to the characters, setting, or plot of the novel. Students are given choice on this activity so that they can decide to complete the activity that most appeals to them. Different multiple intelligences are used so that the activities are diverse and interesting to all students.

How to Use This Literature Guide (cont.)

Culminating Activity

This open-ended, cross-curricular activity requires higher-order thinking and allows for a creative product. Students will enjoy getting the chance to share what they have discovered through reading the novel. Be sure to allow them enough time to complete the activity at school or home.

Comprehension Assessment

The questions in this section are modeled after current standardized tests to help students analyze what they've read and prepare for tests they may see in their classrooms. The questions are dependent on the text and require critical-thinking skills to answer.

Response to Literature

The final post-reading activity is an essay based on the text that also requires further research by students. This is a great way to extend this book into other curricular areas. A suggested rubric is provided for teacher reference.

Correlation to the Standards

Shell Education is committed to producing educational materials that are research and standards based. In this effort, we have correlated all of our products to the academic standards of all 50 United States, the District of Columbia, the Department of Defense Dependents Schools, and all Canadian provinces.

How To Find Standards Correlations

To print a customized correlation report of this product for your state, visit our website at http://www.shelleducation.com and follow the on-screen directions. If you require assistance in printing correlation reports, please contact Customer Service at 1-877-777-3450.

Purpose and Intent of Standards

Standards are designed to focus instruction and guide adoption of curricula. Standards are statements that describe the criteria necessary for students to meet specific academic goals. They define the knowledge, skills, and content students should acquire at each level. Standards are also used to develop standardized tests to evaluate students' academic progress. Teachers are required to demonstrate how their lessons meet standards. Standards are used in the development of all of our products, so educators can be assured they meet high academic standards.

Correlation to the Standards (cont.)

Standards Correlation Chart

The lessons in this guide were written to support the Common Core College and Career Readiness Anchor Standards. This chart indicates which sections of this guide address the anchor standards.

Common Core College and Career Readiness Anchor Standard	Section
CCSS.ELA-Literacy.CCRA.R.1—Read closely to determine what the text says explicitly and to make logical inferences from it; cite specific textual evidence when writing or speaking to support conclusions drawn from the text.	Analyzing the Literature Sections 1–5; Close Reading the Literature Sections 1–5; Creating with the Story Elements Sections 1, 3–5
CCSS.ELA-Literacy.CCRA.R.2—Determine central ideas or themes of a text and analyze their development; summarize the key supporting details and ideas.	Analyzing the Literature Sections 1–5; Close Reading the Literature Sections 1–5; Making Connections Section 5
CCSS.ELA-Literacy.CCRA.R.3—Analyze how and why individuals, events, or ideas develop and interact over the course of a text.	Analyzing the Literature Sections 1–5; Creating with the Story Elements Section 4
CCSS.ELA-Literacy.CCRA.R.4—Interpret words and phrases as they are used in a text, including determining technical, connotative, and figurative meanings, and analyze how specific word choices shape meaning or tone.	Vocabulary Sections 1–5
CCSS.ELA-Literacy.CCRA.R.10—Read and comprehend complex literary and informational texts independently and proficiently.	Entire Unit
CCSS.ELA-Literacy.CCRA.W.1—Write arguments to support claims in an analysis of substantive topics or texts using valid reasoning and relevant and sufficient evidence.	Making Connections Sections 2, 5; Reader Response Sections 1, 3–5; Culminating Activity
CCSS.ELA-Literacy.CCRA.W.2—Write informative/explanatory texts to examine and convey complex ideas and information clearly and accurately through the effective selection, organization, and analysis of content.	Reader Response Sections 1–2, 4; Post-Reading Response to Literature
CCSS.ELA-Literacy.CCRA.W.3—Write narratives to develop real or imagined experiences or events using effective technique, well-chosen details and well-structured event sequences.	Reader Response Sections 2–3, 5; Making Connections Section 4; Creating with the Story Elements Section 4; Culminating Activity
CCSS.ELA-Literacy.CCRA.W.4—Produce clear and coherent writing in which the development, organization, and style are appropriate to task, purpose, and audience.	Making Connections Section 4; Reader Response Sections 1–5; Creating with the Story Elements Section 2; Culminating Activity; Post-Reading Response to Literature

Correlation to the Standards (cont.)

Standards Correlation Chart (cont.)

Common Core College and Career Readiness Anchor Standard	Section
CCSS.ELA-Literacy.CCRA.W.7—Conduct short as well as more sustained research projects based on focused questions, demonstrating understanding of the subject under investigation.	Post-Reading Response to Literature
CCSS.ELA-Literacy.CCRA.SL.1—Prepare for and participate effectively in a range of conversations and collaborations with diverse partners, building on others' ideas and expressing their own clearly and persuasively.	Making Connections Section 5; Analyzing the Literature Sections 1–5
CCSS.ELA-Literacy.CCRA.L.1—Demonstrate command of the conventions of standard English grammar and usage when writing or speaking.	Reader Response Sections 1–5; Close Reading the Literature Sections 1–5; Making Connections Sections 2, 4–5; Creating with the Story Elements Section 2; Culminating Activity
CCSS.ELA-Literacy.CCRA.L.4—Determine or clarify the meaning of unknown and multiple-meaning words and phrases by using context clues, analyzing meaningful word parts, and consulting general and specialized reference materials, as appropriate.	Vocabulary Sections 1–5
CCSS.ELA-Literacy.CCRA.L.6—Acquire and use accurately a range of general academic and domain-specific words and phrases sufficient for reading, writing, speaking, and listening at the college and career readiness level; demonstrate independence in gathering vocabulary knowledge when encountering an unknown term important to comprehension or expression.	Vocabulary Sections 1–5

TESOL and WIDA Standards

The lessons in this book promote English language development for English language learners. The following TESOL and WIDA English Language Development Standards are addressed through the activities in this book:

- **Standard 1:** English language learners communicate for social and instructional purposes within the school setting.

- **Standard 2:** English language learners communicate information, ideas and concepts necessary for academic success in the content area of language arts.

About the Author—Lois Lowry

Lois Lowry is a children's author who has been presented with dozens of awards and has twice received the prestigious Newbery Award for her books *Number the Stars* and *The Giver*.

Born Lois Hammersberg on March 20, 1937, to an army-dentist father and homemaker mother, Lowry has lived all over the United States. She even spent her middle school years in Japan. Her older sister was close to her mother and her younger brother was close to her father, so middle-child Lowry was often alone during her childhood. She enjoyed the solitude, however, and filled the time reading books and writing stories and poems.

After marrying and having four children, Lowry finished college, went on to graduate school, and began writing professionally, which fulfilled her childhood dream. *The Giver* was published in 1993 and won the Newberry Award in 1994. During her acceptance speech, Lowry shared in detail about the many events that slowly trickled into the gushing river that would become the award-winning book. In particular, she shared about her family's time in Japan when she was a young girl. Though living in Tokyo, her family lived in an American community, away from the culture and unfamiliarity of Japan. She attended an American school, watched American movies, and spoke only English to the other Americans she encountered. She loved to explore, though, and would often ride her bike beyond the gate and observe the Japanese men, women, and children. As an adult, she asked her mother why they chose to live in the American village. Her mother explained it was familiar and safe. This idea of sameness versus diversity is seen repeatedly in *The Giver*.

Lowry lives in Cambridge, Massachusetts. She enjoys spending time with her grandchildren and, of course, writing.

Check out her website: http://www.loislowry.com!

Possible Texts for Text Comparisons

Other books written by Lowry include: *Number the Stars*, *Summer to Die*, *Anastasia Krupnik*, and three companion novels to *The Giver* called *Gathering Blue*, *Messenger*, and *Son*. Though her books vary greatly by genre and topics, she feels all of her books have the important theme of human relationships.

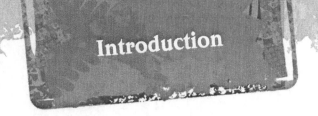

Book Summary of *The Giver*

Imagine a world without pain, without poverty, and without war. Now imagine a world without choice, without love, and without freedom. All of this is the life Jonas lives. For the people in his community, every decision from how they wear their hair to whom they will marry to what their career will be is determined by the governing elders. Everyone is safe, healthy, and under control.

As the Ceremony of Twelve approaches, Jonas is concerned. He, along with all of the other eleven-year-olds, will be given his career assignment. Though Jonas enjoys volunteering in a variety of different jobs, he does not feel a particular interest or passion for any of them. At the ceremony, Jonas and the other citizens are surprised when he is chosen to be the next Receiver of Memory.

Through his training with The Giver, Jonas receives memories of a world he never knew existed. He learns about beautiful things like grandparents, birthdays, and sled rides. But he is also exposed to war, pain, and hunger for the first time. As Jonas gathers more truth and knowledge of the way things were, he begins to ask himself, "Is it better to be free or to be safe?"

Cross-Curricular Connection

This book can be used in a social studies unit on government or a literature study of dystopian societies.

Possible Texts for Text Sets

- Collins, Suzanne. *The Hunger Games*. Scholastic Press, 2010.
- DuPrau, Jeanne. *The City of Ember*. Random House, 2003.
- Haddox, Margaret Peterson. *Among the Hidden*. Simon & Schuster Children's Publishing, 1998.
- Meyer, Marissa. *Cinder*. Square Fish, 2012.
- Roth, Veronica. *Divergent*. Katherine Tegen Books, 2011.

or

- Bowman, David. *What Would the Founding Fathers Think?* Cedar Fort, Inc., 2012.
- Brown, Corinne. *Declaring Our Independence*. Teacher Created Materials, 2006.
- Sobel, Syl. *How the U.S. Government Works*. Barron's Educational Series, 1999.

Name _____

Date _____

Pre-Reading Theme Thoughts

Directions: Read each of the statements in the first column. Decide if you agree or disagree with the statements. Record your opinion by marking an X in Agree or Disagree for each statement. Explain your choices in the third column. There are no right or wrong answers.

Statement	Agree	Disagree	Explain Your Answer
It is better to be safe than to be free.			
The government should protect the people.			
It is okay to forget painful memories and experiences.			
People will always make the right decisions for themselves.			

Vocabulary Overview

Ten key words from this section are provided below with definitions and sentences about how the words are used in the book. Choose one of the vocabulary activity sheets (pages 15 or 16) for students to complete as they read this section. Monitor students as they work to ensure the definitions they have found are accurate and relate to the text. Finally, discuss these important vocabulary words with students. If you think these words or other words in the section warrant more time devoted to them, there are suggestions in the introduction for other vocabulary activities (page 5).

Word	Definition	Sentence about Text
intrigued (ch. 1)	interested	The children are **intrigued** by the planes that bring supplies.
ironic (ch. 1)	strange or funny because it is the opposite of what one might think	The voice says the pilot will be released in an **ironic** tone.
palpable (ch. 1)	obvious, noticeable	Jonas feels **palpable** terror when the plane flies overhead.
transgression (ch. 1)	something that is against the rules	If there is a third **transgression**, the person must be released.
enhance (ch. 2)	to improve	Father hopes calling the newchild by his name will **enhance** his nurturing.
chastise (ch. 3)	to criticize harshly	Jonas waits for his father to **chastise** Lily for saying something rude.
petulantly (ch. 3)	angry or annoyed about not getting one's own way	Lily says she would like to be a birthmother in a **petulant** voice.
conviction (ch. 3)	strong belief or opinion	Jonas has a **conviction** something has happened to the apple.
bypass (ch. 4)	to avoid something by going around it	The talented student will be allowed to **bypass** beginning training.
chortled (ch. 4)	laughed; chuckled	The old woman **chortles** at what Jonas says.

Name _____

Date _____

Understanding Vocabulary Words

Directions: The following words are in this section of the book. Use context clues and reference materials to determine an accurate definition for each word.

Word	Definition
intrigued (ch. 1)	
ironic (ch. 1)	
palpable (ch. 1)	
transgression (ch. 1)	
enhance (ch. 2)	
chastise (ch. 3)	
petulantly (ch. 3)	
conviction (ch. 3)	
bypass (ch. 4)	
chortled (ch. 4)	

Name _____

Date _____

During-Reading Vocabulary Activity

Directions: As you read these chapters, record at least eight important words on the lines below. Try to find interesting, difficult, intriguing, special, or funny words. Your words can be long or short. They can be hard or easy to spell. After each word, use context clues in the text and reference materials to define the word.

- _____
- _____
- _____
- _____
- _____
- _____
- _____
- _____
- _____
- _____

Directions: Respond to these questions about the words in this section.

1. Why does the newchild's growth and progress need to be **enhanced**?

_____

_____

2. Why does Jonas think Lily should be **chastised** by their father?

_____

_____

Analyzing the Literature

Provided below are discussion questions you can use in small groups, with the whole class, or for written assignments. Each question is given at two levels so you can choose the right question for each group of students. Activity sheets with these questions are provided (pages 18–19) if you want students to write their responses. For each question, a few key discussion points are provided for your reference.

Story Element	■ Level 1	▲ Level 2	Key Discussion Points
Character	Describe Jonas, the main character.	Compare Jonas to his groupmates Fiona, Asher, and Benjamin.	Jonas is obedient, very careful with his language, and unsure of what his assignment will be. While Jonas feels a little lost, his friends and other groupmates seem to have strong passions that give a clue as to what their assignments might be.
Setting	How is the community in the book different from your own?	Does this community seem possible? Why or why not?	Two major differences include that the community assigns spouses and children and that the community assigns different responsibilities at various ages (e.g., twelve-year-olds are given their career assignments). Students may or may not think it is possible but explaining their reasoning is important.
Plot	Why does Jonas take the apple?	What do you predict will happen to the apple Jonas takes?	Jonas takes the apple because it seems to change while playing catch with Asher. Students might be able to predict that Jonas sees its true color because the story notes after the apple changes, its shade looks the same as his tunic again.
Character	Describe how Jonas's parents are different.	Describe how Jonas's parents seem to balance each other in their family unit.	Father is very nurturing, sympathetic, and kind. Mother is intelligent, fair, and a rule follower. The committee chose them as spouses because their differences complement each other.

Name _____

Date _____

Analyzing the Literature

Directions: Think about the section you have just read. Read each question and state your response with textual evidence.

1. Describe Jonas, the main character.

_____

_____

_____

_____

2. How is the community in the book different from your own?

_____

_____

_____

_____

3. Why does Jonas take the apple?

_____

_____

_____

_____

4. Describe how Jonas's parents are different.

_____

_____

_____

_____

Name _____

Date _____

▲ Analyzing the Literature

Directions: Think about the section you have just read. Read each question and state your response with textual evidence.

1. Compare Jonas to his groupmates Fiona, Asher, and Benjamin.

_____

_____

_____

_____

2. Does this community seem possible? Why or why not?

_____

_____

_____

_____

3. What do you predict will happen to the apple Jonas takes?

_____

_____

_____

_____

4. Describe how Jonas's parents seem to balance each other in their family unit.

_____

_____

_____

_____

Name _____

Date _____

Reader Response

Directions: Choose one of the following prompts about this section to answer. Be sure to include a topic sentence in your response, use textual evidence to support your opinion, and provide a strong conclusion that summarizes your opinion.

Writing Prompts

- **Opinion/Argument Piece**—Which way of having a family meal is better, how Jonas's family eats or how your family eats? Include examples of what makes your choice better.
- **Informative/Explanatory Piece**—What questions are forming in your mind about the community at this point? Write at least two and explain why you are curious about the answers.

_____

_____

_____

_____

_____

_____

_____

_____

_____

_____

_____

_____

_____

_____

Name _____

Date _____

Close Reading the Literature

Directions: Closely reread the section in chapter 1 where Father describes the newchild, "He's a sweet little male" until the family comforts Mother after she shares her feelings, "Lily stood up and went to her mother." Read each question and then revisit the text to find evidence that supports your answer.

1. For what reasons might someone be released in the community?

   _____

   _____

   _____

   _____

2. Use the text to explain why Father wants to bring the newchild, Gabriel, to their home.

   _____

   _____

   _____

   _____

3. Give evidence from the text about why Mother feels so upset about her day at the Department of Justice.

   _____

   _____

   _____

   _____

4. Based on this scene, what do you think being released means?

   _____

   _____

   _____

   _____

Name _____

Date _____

Making Connections–Child Development

The growth and learning of babies is called child development. There are approximate ages by which babies should have learned certain skills. Those skills are divided into four categories:

- **gross motor**—tasks that use large muscle groups like arms, legs, and torso
- **fine motor**—tasks that use the small muscles of the hands
- **language**—verbally or nonverbally communicating with others
- **social**—interacting with others

Directions: The list below includes skills that most one-year-olds are able to do. Create a four-column chart on another sheet of paper. Label the columns with the four categories above. Sort each skill into the correct category in your chart.

scribbles with a crayon	coos/laughs	feeds self with hands
sits up alone	crawls	picks up objects with thumb and finger
imitates sounds	understands "no"	plays games like peek-a-boo
smiles	responds to name	walks around furniture holding on

Name _____

Date _____

Creating with the Story Elements

Directions: Thinking about the story elements of character, setting, and plot in a novel is very important to understanding what is happening and why. Complete **one** of the following activities about what you've read so far. Be creative and have fun!

Characters

Make a Venn diagram comparing and contrasting Jonas to another character from chapters 1–4. Each character should have at least five details about their differences. The overlapping section should have at least three details about what they have in common. Use the novel to write detailed, thoughtful ideas.

Setting

Draw a map of Jonas's community. Use the text for the names of different locations. A few examples are: Jonas's house, school, Childcare Center, Nurturing Center, Hall of Open Records, and House of the Old. Make sure your map is detailed and clearly labeled so others know what it is.

Plot

Create an assignment poster for the community. The poster should have four sections. Choose an assignment for each section and brainstorm at least three characteristics a person should have to be successful at each job. Make sure the poster is colorful and will grab people's attention.

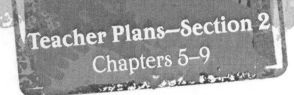

Vocabulary Overview

Ten key words from this section are provided below with definitions and sentences about how the words are used in the book. Choose one of the vocabulary activity sheets (pages 25 or 26) for students to complete as they read this section. Monitor the students as they work to ensure the definitions they have found are accurate and relate to the text. Finally, discuss these important vocabulary words with the students. If you think these words or other words in the section warrant more time devoted to them, there are suggestions in the introduction for other vocabulary activities (page 5).

Word	Definition	Sentence about Text
infraction (ch. 5)	an action that breaks a law or rule	Mother has a dream that she is chastised for a rule **infraction** she does not understand.
reprieve (ch. 6)	a delay that keeps something bad from happening	Gabriel is given a special **reprieve** from the committee and is granted more time.
infringed (ch. 6)	wrongly limited or restrained something	The boy's errors **infringe** on the community's sense of order and success.
meticulously (ch. 6)	doing something in a very exact and careful way	The community is so **meticulously** ordered, Jonas can't imagine anyone being unhappy.
aptitude (ch. 7)	a natural ability to do or learn something	One Twelve has an unusual scientific **aptitude**.
acquisition (ch. 7)	gaining or learning something	The elder shares humorous stories of Asher's language **acquisition**.
integrity (ch. 8)	being honest and fair	**Integrity** is a quality necessary for the new Receiver of Memory.
rigorous (ch. 8)	very demanding with attention to detail	Only the Receiver has undergone the **rigorous** training required.
magnitude (ch. 8)	the size or importance of something	Jonas will be faced with a **magnitude** of pain that the others cannot comprehend.
integral (ch. 9)	very necessary and important	Never telling a lie is an **integral** part of learning the precision of speech.

Name

Date

Understanding Vocabulary Words

Directions: The following words are in this section of the book. Use context clues and reference materials to determine an accurate definition for each word.

Word	Definition
infraction (ch. 5)	
reprieve (ch. 6)	
infringed (ch. 6)	
meticulously (ch. 6)	
aptitude (ch. 7)	
acquisition (ch. 7)	
integrity (ch. 8)	
rigorous (ch. 8)	
magnitude (ch. 8)	
integral (ch. 9)	

Name _____

Date _____

During-Reading Vocabulary Activity

Directions: As you read these chapters, record at least eight important words on the lines below. Try to find interesting, difficult, intriguing, special, or funny words. Your words can be long or short. They can be hard or easy to spell. After each word, use context clues in the text and reference materials to define the word.

- _____
- _____
- _____
- _____
- _____
- _____
- _____
- _____
- _____

Directions: Respond to these questions about the words in this section.

1. According to the text, how are the elders **meticulous** in choosing each new Twelve's assignment?

   _____

   _____

2. How has Jonas already shown that he has **integrity**?

   _____

   _____

Analyzing the Literature

Provided below are discussion questions you can use in small groups, with the whole class, or for written assignments. Each question is given at two levels so you can choose the right question for each group of students. Activity sheets with these questions are provided (pages 28–29) if you want students to write their responses. For each question, a few key discussion points are provided for your reference.

Story Element	■ Level 1	▲ Level 2	Key Discussion Points
Plot	Why does Jonas begin taking a pill every morning?	Why do you think the community does not want the people to have Stirrings?	Jonas begins having Stirrings, feelings of attraction for the opposite gender. The pills stop this feeling. Students' ideas will vary, but they might include that people are easier to control and keep happy if their emotions are suppressed.
Plot	How does the audience feel when Jonas is skipped in the Ceremony of Twelve?	What clues does the author give to show how the audience feels when Jonas is skipped in the Ceremony of Twelve?	The audience is confused, upset, and even a little embarrassed. The clues the author gives are describing the people as shifting in their seats, glancing at Jonas and looking quickly away, and not applauding as loudly at the end.
Character	What five qualities must the Receiver of Memory possess?	How has Jonas already shown he possesses a few of the qualities the Receiver of Memory must possess?	The Receiver must have: intelligence, integrity, courage, wisdom, and the Capacity to See Beyond. Students' opinions will vary, but may include intelligence (his precise language), integrity (apologizing for taking the apple), and Capacity to See Beyond (the examples of the apple and faces in the crowd).
Plot	Which of Jonas's Receiver of Memory Rules is most shocking to him?	Why does Jonas find one of the Receiver of Memory Rules so shocking?	The most surprising rule is the last rule stating he can lie. He is shocked because being truthful is at the core of their entire community. Jonas begins to wonder if the other adults have permission to lie, too, and he has never known.

Name _____

Date _____

Analyzing the Literature

Directions: Think about the section you have just read. Read each question and state your response with textual evidence.

1. Why does Jonas begin taking a pill every morning?

_____

_____

_____

_____

2. How does the audience feel when Jonas is skipped in the Ceremony of Twelve?

_____

_____

_____

_____

3. What five qualities must the Receiver of Memory possess?

_____

_____

_____

_____

4. Which of Jonas's Receiver of Memory Rules is most shocking to him?

_____

_____

_____

_____

Name _____

Date _____

▲ Analyzing the Literature

Directions: Think about the section you have just read. Read each question and state your response with textual evidence.

1. Why do you think the community does not want the people to have Stirrings?

   _____

   _____

   _____

   _____

2. What clues does the author give to show how the audience feels when Jonas is skipped in the Ceremony of Twelve?

   _____

   _____

   _____

   _____

3. How has Jonas already shown he possesses a few of the qualities the Receiver of Memory must possess?

   _____

   _____

   _____

   _____

4. Why does Jonas find one of the Receiver of Memory Rules so shocking?

   _____

   _____

   _____

Name _____

Date _____

Reader Response

Directions: Choose one of the following prompts about this section to answer. Be sure to include a topic sentence in your response, use textual evidence to support your opinion, and provide a strong conclusion that summarizes your opinion.

Writing Prompts

- **Informative/Explanatory Piece**—Jonas is different from his peers in both small and large ways. In what ways do you feel different from your peers?
- **Narrative Piece**—Discuss the problems that you think Jonas will face in his new role as the Receiver. Offer him some advice for how to transition into his new position.

_____

_____

_____

_____

_____

_____

_____

_____

_____

_____

_____

_____

_____

_____

_____

Name _____

Date _____

Close Reading the Literature

Directions: Closely reread the section in chapter 8 when the Chief Elder begins listing the qualities the Receiver must have, "He has shown all of the qualities that a Receiver must have." Continue reading until the end of the chapter. Read each question and then revisit the text to find the evidence that supports your answer.

1. For what reasons will Jonas need courage?

   _____

   _____

   _____

   _____

2. What happens in the book that makes Jonas believe he has the Capacity to See Beyond?

   _____

   _____

   _____

   _____

3. Use the text to explain the symbolism behind the crowd chanting Jonas's name.

   _____

   _____

   _____

   _____

4. According to the text, how does Jonas feel at the end of the ceremony?

   _____

   _____

   _____

   _____

Name _____

Date _____

Making Connections—Pedal Power

In Jonas's community, bicycles are very important to children and adults. Children look forward to receiving their bikes at the Ceremony of Nine and have often been taught to ride beforehand by older siblings or friends.

Directions: Imagine a local school is considering the following idea: *Our school will stop all bus service. Students should ride their bicycles to school.* Brainstorm a list of at least four advantages and four disadvantages of this idea. Choose the side you agree with, and use another piece of paper to write a paragraph supporting your opinion. Your paragraph should have an introduction sentence that states your opinion, supporting details, and a conclusion sentence.

Advantages	Disadvantages

Name _____

Date _____

Creating with the Story Elements

Directions: Thinking about the story elements of character, setting, and plot in a novel is very important to understanding what is happening and why. Complete **one** of the following activities about what you've read so far. Be creative and have fun!

Characters

As the new Twelves are given their assignments, the Elders share stories about their childhoods. Think about Fiona's character traits and make up a story about her youth that might have led the elders to assign her as a Caretaker of the Old. Use your imagination, but also use the information given about Fiona in the text.

Setting

Most of this section takes place in the auditorium during the ceremonies. Draw the auditorium and the children awaiting their ceremony. Label the children according to their age groups. Use details given in the book about the different ages. For example, the Sixes could have jackets with the buttons on the back and the Tens could have their new, short haircuts.

Plot

After Jonas is assigned, he receives a list of rules as the new Receiver of Memory. Think about a job you might like to have as an adult. Make a list of ten rules that would be important to follow in that career.

Vocabulary Overview

Ten key words from this section are provided below with definitions and sentences about how the words are used in the book. Choose one of the vocabulary activity sheets (pages 35 or 36) for students to complete as they read this section. Monitor the students as they work to ensure the definitions they have found are accurate and relate to the text. Finally, discuss these important vocabulary words with the students. If you think these words or other words in the section warrant more time devoted to them, there are suggestions in the introduction for other vocabulary activities.

Word	Definition	Sentence about Text
intricate (ch. 10)	very detailed, with many parts	The bed is draped with a cloth embroidered with **intricate** designs.
transmit (ch. 10)	to pass from one person to another	The Giver's job is to **transmit** all of the memories within him.
tentatively (ch. 10)	to do something without confidence	Jonas **tentatively** says he would be interested in hearing about the Receiver's life.
torrent (ch. 11)	a large amount of something that is released all at once	He can see a bright, whirling **torrent** of crystals in the air around him.
perceive (ch. 11)	to learn or become aware of something	Jonas should be able to **perceive** the names without being told.
admonition (ch. 12)	a warning about behavior	Jonas is aware of the rules' **admonition** not to discuss his training.
relinquished (ch. 12)	gave up something	The community **relinquished** color when they did away with differences.
sinuous (ch. 13)	having twists and turns	With its **sinuous** trunk, the elephant strokes the huge corpse.
exempted (ch. 13)	not required to do something others are	Although Jonas is **exempted** from the rules against rudeness, he knows his question is rude.
subsided (ch. 13)	became less intense	The pain of the memories **subsides** over time.

Name

Date

Understanding Vocabulary Words

Directions: The following words are in this section of the book. Use context clues and reference materials to determine an accurate definition for each word.

Word	Definition
intricate (ch. 10)	
transmit (ch. 10)	
tentatively (ch. 10)	
torrent (ch. 11)	
perceive (ch. 11)	
admonition (ch. 12)	
relinquished (ch. 12)	
sinuous (ch. 13)	
exempted (ch. 13)	
subsided (ch. 13)	

Name _____

Date _____

During-Reading Vocabulary Activity

Directions: As you read these chapters, record at least eight important words on the lines below. Try to find interesting, difficult, intriguing, special, or funny words. Your words can be long or short. They can be hard or easy to spell. After each word, use context clues in the text and reference materials to define the word.

- _____

- _____

- _____

- _____

- _____

- _____

- _____

- _____

- _____

- _____

Directions: Now, organize your words. Rewrite each of your words on a sticky note. Work as a group to create a bar graph of your words. You should stack any words that are the same on top of one another. Different words appear in different columns. Finally, discuss with your teacher why certain words were chosen more often than other words.

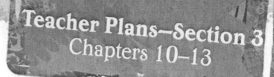

Analyzing the Literature

Provided below are discussion questions you can use in small groups, with the whole class, or for written assignments. Each question is given at two levels so you can choose the right question for each group of students. Activity sheets with these questions are provided (pages 38–39) if you want students to write their responses. For each question, a few key discussion points are provided for your reference.

Story Element	■ Level 1	▲ Level 2	Key Discussion Points
Setting	Describe The Giver's room in the Annex.	Compare and contrast The Giver's room and Jonas's dwelling.	The Giver's room has fancy furniture, colorful bed coverings, and shelves of books. Jonas's dwelling has plain furniture and only the three standard books of the community.
Character	Describe The Giver.	How is The Giver different from other adults in the community?	The Giver is old and wise, with light eyes like Jonas's. He is somewhat sad, weighted down with memories. Unlike other adults, he encourages questions, does not require apologies, and does not think the instructors know everything.
Plot	In what way is Jonas able to see beyond?	What clues led The Giver to believe Jonas could see beyond?	Jonas is able to see the color red. The Giver figures this out because the apple Jonas took and Fiona's hair are red, as well as the red tones in the faces of the audience members at the ceremony.
Character	With whom does Jonas try to share memories, and what memories are they?	Why do you think Jonas wants to share the memories?	Jonas tries to share colors with Asher and tries to share the elephant with his father and Lily. Students' answers will vary, but they may include that Jonas feels frustrated that others do not know what he does. He wants to share his new awareness of these beautiful things with his family and friends.

Name _____

Date _____

Analyzing the Literature

Directions: Think about the section you have just read. Read each question and state your response with textual evidence.

1. Describe The Giver's room in the Annex.

_____

_____

_____

_____

2. Describe The Giver.

_____

_____

_____

_____

3. In what way is Jonas able to see beyond?

_____

_____

_____

_____

4. With whom does Jonas try to share memories, and what memories are they?

_____

_____

_____

_____

Name _____

Date _____

▲ Analyzing the Literature

Directions: Think about the section you have just read. Read each question and state your response with textual evidence.

1. Compare and contrast The Giver's room and Jonas's dwelling.

   _____

   _____

   _____

   _____

2. How is The Giver different from other adults in the community?

   _____

   _____

   _____

   _____

3. What clues led The Giver to believe Jonas could see beyond?

   _____

   _____

   _____

   _____

4. Why do you think Jonas wants to share the memories?

   _____

   _____

   _____

   _____

Name _____

Date _____

Reader Response

Directions: Choose one of the following prompts about this section to answer. Be sure you include a topic sentence in your response, use textual evidence to support your opinion, and provide a strong conclusion that summarizes your opinion.

Writing Prompts

- **Narrative Piece**—Jonas is starting to question the choices of the community. Tell about a time when you fought for something that was important to you.
- **Opinion/Argument Piece**—What have you learned about Jonas in this section that you think will be important later in the novel?

_____

_____

_____

_____

_____

_____

_____

_____

_____

_____

_____

_____

_____

_____

_____

_____

Name _____

Date _____

Close Reading the Literature

Directions: Closely reread the section at the beginning of chapter 13 when Jonas and The Giver are talking about Sameness. Start when Jonas says, "But I want them!" Continue reading until they finish their conversation with, "Jonas was left, still, with . . ." Read each question and then revisit the text to find the evidence that supports your answer.

1. What text evidence helps the reader understand why Jonas thinks that not having colors is unfair?

   _____

   _____

   _____

   _____

2. According to the text, which decisions are too important for people to make themselves?

   _____

   _____

   _____

   _____

3. When Jonas states that Sameness is safer, what examples does he give for what might go wrong if people had choices?

   _____

   _____

   _____

   _____

4. The Giver agrees that Sameness is safer. How can you use the text to determine if The Giver is stating his true opinion?

   _____

   _____

   _____

   _____

Name _____

Date _____

Making Connections—Make a Terrarium

Jonas's community has climate control, which does not have sunshine or rain. They are able to grow crops in alternative ways. This can be modeled with a terrarium. Build a terrarium of your own and observe the way food can be grown indoors.

Materials

- 2-liter soft drink bottle
- water
- potting soil
- pebbles
- seeds (lima beans, bell peppers, carrots, soy beans)
- duct tape
- fluorescent light

Procedure

1. Cut off the bottom third of the soda bottle. Make two one-inch slits around the bottom of the top section and put it aside.
2. Place a layer of pebbles in the base of the bottle.
3. Add a layer of potting soil on top of the pebbles.
4. Plant three to five seeds one-half to one inch below soil level.
5. Add just enough water to moisten the soil.
6. Place the top of the bottle back onto the bottom, sliding the slits down onto the base. Seal tightly with duct tape.
7. Place the terrarium directly under fluorescent lights.
8. Observe and monitor plant progress for several weeks.

Response

1. Why is the fluorescent light necessary?

   _____

   _____

   _____

2. Which seeds do you think will grow the fastest? Why?

   _____

   _____

   _____

Name _____

Date _____

Creating with the Story Elements

Directions: Thinking about the story elements of character, setting, and plot in a novel is very important to understanding what is happening and why. Complete **one** of the following activities about what you've read so far. Be creative and have fun!

Characters

Choose a memory Jonas has received from The Giver and draw a picture of it. Use the text to add details.

Setting

When Jonas visits The Giver for the first time, he is surprised that although they have the same kinds of furniture, The Giver's is very different. Use text details, along with your imagination, to draw what The Giver's room and Jonas's dwelling might look like.

Plot

Create a T-chart and label the two sections **Positive Memories** and **Negative Memories**. Sort the memories Jonas has received so far in the chart. Then, predict at least five more memories The Giver might share with Jonas and write them in the correct sections.

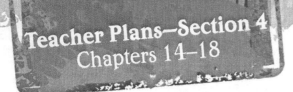

Vocabulary Overview

Ten key words from this section are provided below with definitions and sentences about how the words are used in the book. Choose one of the vocabulary activity sheets (pages 45 or 46) for students to complete as they read this section. Monitor the students as they work to ensure the definitions they have found are accurate and relate to the text. Finally, discuss these important vocabulary words with the students. If you think these words or other words in the section warrant more time devoted to them, there are suggestions in the introduction for other vocabulary activities.

Word	Definition	Sentence about Text
assuage (ch. 14)	to make something less painful	It is not enough to **assuage** the pain Jonas is experiencing.
excruciating (ch. 14)	very painful	The hunger causes **excruciating** pain in his stomach.
ominous (ch. 14)	feeling that something bad is going to happen	The phrase, "back and back and back" is **ominous**.
placidly (ch. 14)	not easily upset	Gabriel is **placidly** hugging his hippo while in the crib.
contorted (ch. 15)	twisted into an unusual shape	The Giver's face is **contorted** with pain and suffering.
solitude (ch. 16)	being alone by choice	Jonas gains an understanding of **solitude** and its joy.
pervaded (ch. 16)	spreading throughout all parts of something	Jonas feels the happiness that **pervaded** the memory.
horde (ch. 17)	a large group	A **horde** of children run from their hiding places during their warfare game.
luminous (ch. 18)	seeming to produce light	The Giver remembers the girl's eyes were **luminous**.
successor (ch. 18)	a person who has a job after someone else	The Giver needs a **successor**, and Jonas has been chosen.

Name _____

Date _____

Understanding Vocabulary Words

Directions: The following words are in this section of the book. Use context clues and reference materials to determine an accurate definition for each word.

Word	Definition
assuage (ch. 14)	
excruciating (ch. 14)	
ominous (ch. 14)	
placidly (ch. 14)	
contorted (ch. 15)	
solitude (ch. 16)	
pervaded (ch. 16)	
horde (ch. 17)	
luminous (ch. 18)	
successor (ch. 18)	

Name _____

Date _____

During-Reading Vocabulary Activity

Directions: As you read these chapters, record at least eight important words on the lines below. Try to find interesting, difficult, intriguing, special, or funny words. Your words can be long or short. They can be hard or easy to spell. After each word, use context clues in the text and reference materials to define the word.

- _____
- _____
- _____
- _____
- _____
- _____
- _____
- _____
- _____
- _____

Directions: Respond to these questions about the words in this section.

1. Why does Jonas begin to think the phrase, "back and back and back" is **ominous**?

   _____

   _____

2. How does **solitude** bring Jonas joy in the memories?

   _____

   _____

   _____

Analyzing the Literature

Provided below are discussion questions you can use in small groups, with the whole class, or for written assignments. Each question is given at two levels so you can choose the right question for each group of students. Activity sheets with these questions are provided (pages 48–49) if you want students to write their responses. For each question, a few key discussion points are provided for your reference.

Story Element	■ Level 1	▲ Level 2	Key Discussion Points
Character	What is Jonas's first experience with true pain?	What is different about Jonas's pain in the sledding memory compared to his real life?	Jonas's first experience with pain is the memory of the sled crash and breaking his leg. This pain lasts longer than usual, and he is not allowed to request relief-of-pain medication like he can in the community.
Plot	What happens when Gabriel sleeps in Jonas's room?	How do you think Gabriel receiving memories will impact the story?	Jonas secretly transmits memories to Gabriel to help him sleep more soundly. Students' predictions will vary, but examples are: Gabriel becomes a second Receiver; The Giver finds out and is angry; or Gabriel is released and his memories escape into the community like before.
Setting	Describe The Giver's favorite memory.	Why does Jonas feel conflicted about The Giver's favorite memory?	The Giver's favorite memory is of a family with grandparents gathering together at a holiday. Jonas is conflicted because he enjoys the memory and the feeling of love, but he still clings to the community's belief that it isn't very practical to mix generations or celebrate in ways that might be risky or dangerous.
Plot	Who is Rosemary, and what happened to her?	Why would the loss of Jonas be more devastating for the community than the loss of Rosemary?	Before Jonas, Rosemary was the Receiver who failed. She requested release to Elsewhere after five weeks of working with The Giver and receiving memories of loneliness and loss. After her release, the memories she had were let loose on the community, and the people were in turmoil. Jonas has been the Receiver for a year, so if he is lost, there would be many more memories released to the community.

Name _____

Date _____

Analyzing the Literature

Directions: Think about the section you have just read. Read each question and state your response with textual evidence.

1. What is Jonas's first experience with true pain?

   _____

   _____

   _____

   _____

2. What happens when Gabriel sleeps in Jonas's room?

   _____

   _____

   _____

   _____

3. Describe The Giver's favorite memory.

   _____

   _____

   _____

   _____

4. Who is Rosemary, and what happened to her?

   _____

   _____

   _____

   _____

Name _____

Date _____

▲ Analyzing the Literature

Directions: Think about the section you have just read. Read each question and state your response with textual evidence.

1. What is different about Jonas's pain in the sledding memory compared to his real life?

_____

_____

_____

_____

2. How do you think Gabriel receiving memories will impact the story?

_____

_____

_____

_____

3. Why does Jonas feel conflicted about The Giver's favorite memory?

_____

_____

_____

_____

4. Why would the loss of Jonas be more devastating for the community than the loss of Rosemary?

_____

_____

_____

_____

Name _____

Date _____

Reader Response

Directions: Choose one of the following prompts about this section to answer. Be sure you include a topic sentence in your response, use textual evidence to support your opinion, and provide a strong conclusion that summarizes your opinion.

Writing Prompts

- **Opinion/Argument Piece**—In what ways are you like The Giver or Jonas? Choose one of these characters and compare him to yourself.
- **Informative/Explanatory Piece**—What new pieces of information do you learn about the community in this section? How does that change your opinion of the choices made by the community's leaders?

_____

_____

_____

_____

_____

_____

_____

_____

_____

_____

_____

_____

_____

_____

Name

Date

Close Reading the Literature

Directions: Closely reread the section at the beginning of chapter 17 that starts with, "Psssheeewwww!" Continue reading until Jonas and his friends ride away, "Jonas knew with certainty that he could change nothing." Read each question and then revisit the text to find the evidence that supports your answer.

1. Based on the events in the story, why does the children's game upset Jonas?

_____

_____

_____

2. According to the text, how do the other children react to Jonas?

_____

_____

_____

3. Use the text to explain why Asher gets angry at Jonas.

_____

_____

_____

4. Give evidence from the text to describe what has changed in Jonas's friendships with Asher and Fiona.

_____

_____

_____

Name _____

Date _____

Making Connections–Transmit a Memory

Memories are an important part of this story. The Giver is able to transmit memories simply by placing his hands on Jonas's back. In real life, people must share their memories through words, writing, or pictures.

Directions: Choose a memory from your life. It can be happy, painful, scary, or funny. Attempt to "transmit" your memory through writing. Remember what you saw, heard, and felt so that you can add details to show your ideas and help the reader "receive" your memory. (Hint: Make sure your memory is clear, but small. For example, don't choose an entire vacation at the beach—instead focus on one afternoon of building a sand castle.)

_____

_____

_____

_____

_____

_____

_____

_____

_____

_____

_____

_____

_____

_____

_____

Name

Date

Creating with the Story Elements

Directions: Thinking about the story elements of character, setting, and plot in a novel is very important to understanding what is happening and why. Complete **one** of the following activities about what you've read so far. Be creative and have fun!

Characters

Create a comic strip about the first time Jonas accidentally transmitted a memory to Gabriel. Although the characters do not speak in that scene, use the text and your imagination to create thought bubbles for Jonas and Gabriel.

Setting

Though people in the community have never been to Elsewhere, it is a place often mentioned. Imagine what Jonas thinks Elsewhere looks like and draw it.

Plot

What if Rosemary had not requested release? Make a list of ten things that might be different in the story if she had continued as the Receiver. Think about all of the main characters and how this change would affect them.

Vocabulary Overview

Ten key words from this section are provided below with definitions and sentences about how the words are used in the book. Choose one of the vocabulary activity sheets (pages 55 or 56) for students to complete as they read this section. Monitor students as they work to ensure the definitions they have found are accurate and relate to the text. Finally, discuss these important vocabulary words with students. If you think these words or other words in the section warrant more time devoted to them, there are suggestions in the introduction for other vocabulary activities (page 5).

Word	Definition	Sentence about Text
syringe (ch. 19)	a hollow tube with a needle used for giving shots	Father takes out a **syringe** and a small bottle for the twin's release.
emphatically (ch. 20)	done with emphasis	Jonas shakes his head **emphatically** when The Giver offers to transmit music memories.
solace (ch. 20)	giving comfort	The community does not have memories to give them **solace** or wisdom.
languid (ch. 21)	having little energy	Jonas gives Gabriel a memory with **languid** water lapping at the shore.
augmented (ch. 21)	added to something to complete it	Jonas divides up the food and **augments** it with what he finds in the fields.
vigilant (ch. 21)	noticing signs of danger	Jonas is constantly **vigilant**, looking for their next hiding place.
subtle (ch. 22)	hard to notice	There is a **subtle** change to the landscape that is hard to notice at first.
tantalizing (ch. 22)	interesting or appealing	Jonas tries to remember **tantalizing** meals and banquets.
lethargy (ch. 23)	lack of energy	Warming himself with a memory gets rid of Jonas's **lethargy**.
impeded (ch. 23)	slowed the action of something	Jonas is **impeded** by the snow and his own physical weaknesses.

Name _____

Date _____

Understanding Vocabulary Words

Directions: The following words are in this section of the book. Use context clues and reference materials to determine an accurate definition for each word.

Word	Definition
syringe (ch. 19)	
emphatically (ch. 20)	
solace (ch. 20)	
languid (ch. 21)	
augmented (ch. 21)	
vigilant (ch. 21)	
subtle (ch. 22)	
tantalizing (ch. 22)	
lethargy (ch. 23)	
impeded (ch. 23)	

Name _____

Date _____

During-Reading Vocabulary Activity

Directions: As you read these chapters, choose five important words from the story. Use these words to complete the word flow chart below. On each arrow, write a word. In each box, explain how the connected pair of words relates to each other. An example for the words *vigilant* and *subtle* has been done for you.

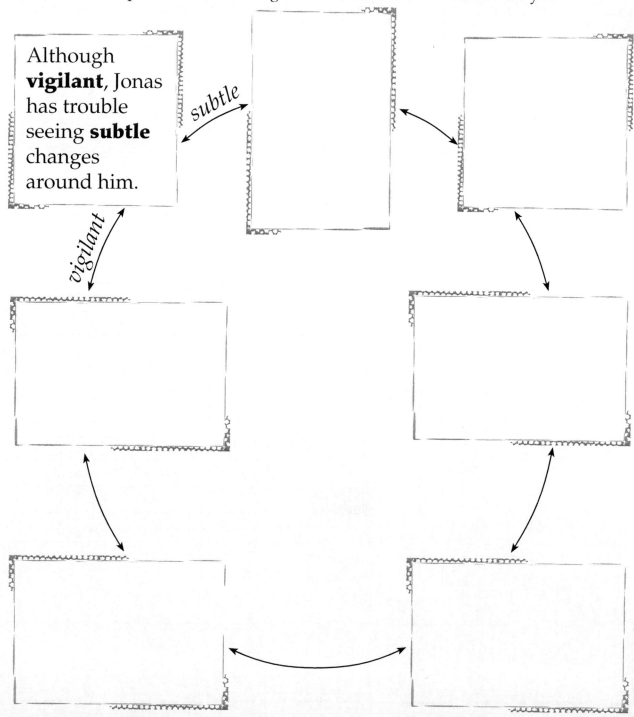

Although **vigilant**, Jonas has trouble seeing **subtle** changes around him.

Analyzing the Literature

Provided below are discussion questions you can use in small groups, with the whole class, or for written assignments. Each question is given at two levels so you can choose the right question for each group of students. Activity sheets with these questions are provided (pages 58–59) if you want students to write their responses. For each question, a few key discussion points are provided for your reference.

Story Element	■ Level 1	▲ Level 2	Key Discussion Points
Plot	What does Jonas discover about release?	What do you think those who do the releasing of others (like Jonas's father) think about it?	Jonas learns that when people are released, they do not go to Elsewhere. They die. Students' answers may include: they don't know any better; they are just doing their job; or they do not understand what dying really is.
Character	What is Jonas's reaction to the discovery about what release is?	How have Jonas's feelings toward his parents changed?	Jonas is furious and so upset he stays with The Giver one night because he does not want to see his father. He now finds it easy to lie to his parents and knows they lie to him as well, even if they do not know better. He seems to lose respect for them.
Plot	What is the original plan for Jonas's escape?	How does Jonas's escape actually end up happening?	The original plan is that Jonas would pretend to be lost in the river, but he would really escape in a truck, full of memories of courage and with plenty of food The Giver has saved for him. Jonas has to leave unexpectedly, earlier than planned to save Gabriel from being released. He takes his father's bike and whatever food he can find and sets off with Gabriel, unable to tell The Giver good-bye.
Setting	Why does the land change as Jonas escapes the community?	In what ways is the setting outside the community different from the community?	The setting changes because he is outside of the community's control. Not everywhere in the world has climate control, just where the community has built it. Jonas encounters hills, cold weather, rain and snow, and sees animals for the first time.

Name _____

Date _____

Analyzing the Literature

Directions: Think about the section you have just read. Read each question and state your response with textual evidence.

1. What does Jonas discover about release?

_____

_____

_____

_____

2. What is Jonas's reaction to the discovery about what release is?

_____

_____

_____

_____

3. What is the original plan for Jonas's escape?

_____

_____

_____

_____

4. Why does the land change as Jonas escapes the community?

_____

_____

_____

_____

Name _____

Date _____

▲ Analyzing the Literature

Directions: Think about the section you have just read. Read each question and state your response with textual evidence.

1. What do you think those who do the releasing of others (like Jonas's father) think about it?

   _____

   _____

   _____

   _____

2. How have Jonas's feelings toward his parents changed?

   _____

   _____

   _____

   _____

3. How does Jonas's escape actually end up happening?

   _____

   _____

   _____

   _____

4. In what ways is the setting outside the community different from the community?

   _____

   _____

   _____

Name _____

Date _____

Reader Response

Directions: Choose one of the following prompts about this section to answer. Be sure you include a topic sentence in your response, use textual evidence to support your opinion, and provide a strong conclusion that summarizes your opinion.

Writing Prompts

- **Narrative Piece**—Finding out the truth about release is shocking to Jonas. Describe a time in your life when you discovered something that truly shocked you.
- **Opinion/Argument Piece**—Give at least three reasons why every student your age should have to read this book.

_____

_____

_____

_____

_____

_____

_____

_____

_____

_____

_____

_____

_____

_____

Name _____

Date _____

Close Reading the Literature

Directions: Closely reread the section in chapter 20 when The Giver and Jonas make their plan. Start with, "It was late at night now." Stop reading when Jonas will not take The Giver's memory, "I want you to keep that, to have with you, when I'm gone." Read each question and then revisit the text to find the evidence that supports your answer.

1. Describe, with text support, what will happen if Jonas leaves the community.

   _____

   _____

   _____

   _____

2. Use text evidence to explain why The Giver is unwilling to go with Jonas.

   _____

   _____

   _____

   _____

3. According to the text, why will the community have to bear the memories?

   _____

   _____

   _____

   _____

4. What memory will Jonas not take from The Giver? Why?

   _____

   _____

   _____

   _____

Name _____

Date _____

Making Connections—The Great Debate

Directions: Use the information below and work with a partner to create your own arguments for a class debate. Be prepared to share your ideas in a mock-debate with your classmates.

A debate is a formal discussion between two people or groups. The topic is usually something that is not agreed upon. In *The Giver*, the idea of Sameness is often addressed. The community thinks Sameness is the right way to live, and Jonas begins to disagree as the story progresses.

1. **Opinion** (Choose Sameness or Differences.)

   _____

2. **Opening** (List reasons or write about the advantages of the side you chose.)

   _____

   _____

   _____

   _____

3. **Attack** (List reasons or write about problems with the other side.)

   _____

   _____

   _____

   _____

4. **Rebuttal** (Think of arguments the other side will make about your choice. Defend your ideas against their attack.)

   _____

   _____

   _____

   _____

Name _____

Date _____

Creating with the Story Elements

Directions: Thinking about the story elements of character, setting, and plot in a novel is very important to understanding what is happening and why. Complete **one** of the following activities about what you've read so far. Be creative and have fun!

Characters

Jonas and Gabriel's journey brings them many new discoveries. Create a T-chart, and list both positive and negative things they experience on their escape from the community.

Setting

Jonas wishes The Giver could have left the community, but he understands why he cannot. Write a letter from Jonas to The Giver describing the world outside of the community.

Plot

Create a visual flowchart for three to five important events in chapter 23. Use the text to add details and images to your graphic organizer

Name _____

Date _____

Post-Reading Theme Thoughts

Directions: Read each of the statements in the first column. Choose a main character from *The Giver*. Think about that character's point of view. From that character's perspective, decide if the character would agree or disagree with the statements. Record the character's opinion by marking an *X* in Agree or Disagree for each statement. Explain your choices in the third column using text evidence.

Character I Chose: _____

Statement	Agree	Disagree	Explain Your Answer
It is better to be safe than to be free.			
The government should protect the people.			
It is okay to forget painful memories and experiences.			
People will always make the right decisions for themselves.			

Name _____

Date _____

Culminating Activity: Chapter 24—My End

Overview: The ending of *The Giver* is very ambiguous, meaning it could be understood in more than one way. This was the intent of the author, Lois Lowry. She even said, "Those of you who hoped I would . . . reveal the 'true' ending . . . will be disappointed. There isn't one. There's a right one for each of us, and it depends on our own beliefs, our own hopes." This idea can be both freeing and frustrating to the readers.

Directions: How do you think the book really ends? Is it happy, sad, or something in-between? What happens to Jonas and Gabriel? What about The Giver and the people in the community? Use the lines below to record your thoughts about the ending.

_____

_____

_____

_____

_____

_____

_____

_____

_____

_____

_____

_____

Name _____

Date _____

Culminating Activity: Chapter 24—My End (cont.)

Directions: When you have completed your description of the ending of *The Giver*, select one of the culminating projects below to complete.

Write your own chapter 24 as a continuation of the book. Try to imitate the author's style of writing. Use your work on the previous page to predict what happens next for Jonas and Gabriel.

Write your own chapter 24 as the final act of a play. The characters should have lines and stage directions.

Write your own chapter 24 as a comic strip. Draw detailed pictures to help explain what is happening and give the characters speech bubbles.

Name _____

Date _____

Comprehension Assessment

Directions: Circle the letter for the best response to each question.

1. What is the meaning of *Sameness* as it is used in the book?

    A. removing color from nature

    B. eliminating differences in the community

    C. assigning jobs to twelve-year-olds

    D. creating people who look identical

2. Which detail from the book best supports your answer to question 1?

    E. "We relinquished sunshine and did away with differences."

    F. "There were a lot of colors and one of them was called red."

    G. "I suppose the genetic scientists are still hard at work trying to work the kinks out."

    H. "I'm going to give you a memory of a rainbow."

3. What is the main idea of the text below?

    "If you get away, if you get beyond, if you get to Elsewhere, it will mean that the community has to bear the burden themselves, of the memories you had been holding for them. I think that they can, and that they will acquire some wisdom. But it will be desperately hard for them . . . When your memories return, they'll need help."

    _____

    _____

    _____

    _____

4. Choose **two** details from those below to support your answer to question 3.

    A. Jonas hides from the search planes.

    B. The memories are growing weaker on Jonas's journey.

    C. Jonas has trouble remembering snow.

    D. The community gives honor to The Giver.

Comprehension Assessment *(cont.)*

5. Which statement best expresses one of the themes of the book?

    E. Laws should be followed.

    F. It is important to fit in.

    G. Friendships are valuable.

    H. People should make their own choices.

6. What detail from the book provides the best evidence for your answer to number 5?

    A. "He felt such love for Asher and Fiona."

    B. "I want to wake up in the morning and decide things!"

    C. "It's what he was told to do, and he knows nothing else."

    D. "But he had taken the apple home, against the recreation area rules."

7. What is the purpose of these sentences from the book: "The worst part of holding the memories is not the pain. It's the loneliness of it. Memories need to be shared."

_____

_____

_____

_____

_____

_____

8. Which other quotation from the story serves a similar purpose?

    E. "He put his hands on Asher's shoulders, and concentrated on the red of the petals, trying to hold it as long as he could, and trying at the same time to transmit the awareness of red to his friend."

    F. "'I am going to transmit the memory of snow,' the old man said, and placed his hands on Jonas's bare back."

    G. "Jonas, you and I are the only ones who have feelings. We've been sharing them now for almost a year."

    H. "Of course they needed to care. It was the meaning of everything."

Name _____

Date _____

Response to Literature:
The Government of *The Giver*

Overview: In *The Giver*, the author creates a community that is contentedly controlled by its government. Throughout history, many different types of governments have been established to both help and oppress its people. Examples of governments include: communist, democracy, socialist, republic, and monarchy.

Directions: Select three different types of government. (They do not have to be on the list above.) Compare and contrast these with the governing structure in *The Giver*. What advantages and disadvantages can be found within each type? Write a research essay that shows your understanding of different types of government and how they relate to the one in the novel. Use facts and examples from your research and also cite the book to support your thinking. In conclusion, explain your opinion on the strengths and weaknesses of the government in *The Giver*.

Your essay response to literature should follow these guidelines:

- Be at least 750 words in length.
- Cite information about three types of government.
- Compare/contrast types of governments with the one in the novel.
- Cite at least three references from the novel.
- Provide a conclusion that summarizes your thoughts and findings.

Final essays are due on _____.

Name _____

Date _____

Response to Literature Rubric

Directions: Use this rubric to evaluate student responses to *The Giver*.

	Exceptional Writing	Quality Writing	Developing Writing
Focus and Organization	☐ States a clear opinion and elaborates well. Engages the reader from hook through the middle to the conclusion. Demonstrates clear understanding of the intended audience and purpose of the piece.	☐ Provides a clear and consistent opinion. Maintains a clear perspective and supports it through elaborating details. Makes the opinion clear in the opening hook and summarizes well in the conclusion.	☐ Provides an inconsistent point of view. Does not support the topic adequately or misses pertinent information. Provides lack of clarity in the beginning, middle, and conclusion.
Text Evidence	☐ Provides comprehensive and accurate support. Includes relevant and worthwhile text references.	☐ Provides limited support. Provides few supporting text references.	☐ Provides very limited support for the text. Provides two or less supporting text references.
Written Expression	☐ Uses descriptive and precise language with clarity and intention. Maintains a consistent voice and uses an appropriate tone that supports meaning. Uses multiple sentence types and transitions well between ideas.	☐ Uses a broad vocabulary. Maintains a consistent voice and supports a tone and feelings through language. Varies sentence length and word choices.	☐ Uses a limited and unvaried vocabulary. Provides an inconsistent or weak voice and tone. Provides little to no variation in sentence type and length.
Language Conventions	☐ Capitalizes, punctuates, and spells accurately. Demonstrates complete thoughts within sentences, with accurate subject-verb agreement. Uses paragraphs appropriately and with clear purpose.	☐ Capitalizes, punctuates, and spells accurately. Demonstrates complete thoughts within sentences and appropriate grammar. Paragraphs are properly divided and supported.	☐ Incorrectly capitalizes, punctuates, and spells. Uses fragmented or run-on sentences. Utilizes poor grammar overall. Paragraphs are poorly divided and developed.

The responses provided here are just examples of what the students may answer. Many accurate responses are possible for the questions throughout this unit.

During-Reading Vocabulary Activity—Section 1:
Chapters 1–4 (page 16)

1. The newchild's growth needs to be **enhanced** because he is not growing at the right rate and is not sleeping well at night.

2. Jonas thinks Lily should be **chastised** because she makes a rude comment about the newchild having strange eyes, like Jonas.

Close Reading the Literature—Section 1:
Chapters 1–4 (page 21)

1. People can be released if they are old, a newchild who is not thriving, or a person who has committed three transgressions.

2. Father wants to bring Gabriel to their home because he feels the child will do better if he is around the family instead of at the Nurturing Center with the underqualified night staff.

3. Mother is upset because there was a man brought before her who had committed his second transgression. She feels guilty she has not done more to help him and scared because he will be released if he commits one more transgression.

4. Examples may include: Being released is dying. Being released is being sent away to live in a different community.

Making Connections—Section 1:
Chapters 1–4 (page 22)

- **Gross Motor**—crawls, sits up alone, walks around furniture holding on
- **Fine Motor**—feeds self with hands, picks up objects with thumb and finger, scribbles with a crayon
- **Language**—coos/laughs, imitates sounds, understands "no," responds to name
- **Social**—plays games like peek-a-boo, smiles

During-Reading Vocabulary Activity—Section 2:
Chapters 5–9 (page 26)

1. The elders are **meticulous** because they spend hours observing the children during their volunteer hours to discover where their talents and passions lie.

2. Jonas shows **integrity** because he immediately apologizes and takes responsibility for his mistake when he hears the announcement directed to him about not removing food from the cafeteria.

Close Reading the Literature—Section 2:
Chapters 5–9 (page 31)

1. Jonas will need courage because becoming the Receiver will cause him to experience physical pain, which he has never had to endure.

2. Jonas thinks he may have the Capacity to See Beyond when the faces in the crowd change for an instant, just like the apple.

3. The crowd chanting Jonas's name symbolizes their accepting him in his new role and giving him new life as the Receiver.

4. Jonas feels gratitude and pride, but he is also afraid because he does not know what will happen to him.

Making Connections—Section 2:
Chapters 5–9 (page 32)

Students' answers will vary, but may include:

- **Advantages**—less pollution, good exercise, less expensive for school because the buses will not run, avoid bullying and fighting on the bus
- **Disadvantages**—severe weather will make riding difficult, possibility of bike theft, dangerous if there are major intersections, no alternative solution for students with physical disabilities

Close Reading the Literature—Section 3:
Chapters 10–13 (page 41)

1. Jonas thinks getting rid of colors is unfair because people do not have choices when everything is the same. He gives examples of choosing what color tunic to wear and what toy Gabriel can choose to play with.

2. The important decisions Jonas feels people should not make on their own are choosing a spouse and their job assignment.

3. Jonas feels people could make the wrong decision for themselves, which would be frightening and problematic. He wants to protect people from wrong choices. Specifically, he worries about choosing mates and jobs.

4. Students can support either answer: The Giver does agree with Jonas because he has the wisdom of past problems and thinks Sameness is the answer. The Giver does not really agree with Jonas, but says he does because Jonas is not ready to realize the truth yet.

Making Connections—Section 3:
Chapters 10–13 (page 42)

1. The fluorescent light is necessary because there is no sunlight for the plants, and they need a light source.

2. Student responses will vary.

During-Reading Vocabulary Activity—Section 4:
Chapters 14–18 (page 46)

1. The phrase becomes **ominous** to Jonas because he realizes that nothing will change; it has been this way for so long, no one knows differently or wants change.

2. Jonas learns about the joy of **solitude** through activities like walking in the woods and sitting by a campfire.

Close Reading the Literature—Section 4:
Chapters 14–18 (page 51)

1. The game upsets Jonas because he recognizes it as a war game for the first time, and now he understands what war is.

2. The other children are confused by his reaction. The text says they stare at him uncertainly, and eventually they get on their bikes and leave.

3. Asher is upset because he is enjoying the game. As he is training for Assistant to the Recreation Director, he feels he should have the authority over what the children play.

4. Jonas's friendships with Asher and Fiona are changing because they do not have the depth of feeling he is gaining. He feels love for them, but they are not able to feel it back. Their lives are unchanged, but Jonas has memories now and has trouble relating to his old friends.

Making Connections—Section 4:
Chapters 14–18 (page 52)

Student responses will vary. Look to see that students are "showing" rather than "telling" their memories.

Close Reading the Literature—Section 5:
Chapters 19–23 (page 61)

1. If Jonas leaves the community, the memories he received will come back to the people.

2. The Giver is unwilling to leave with Jonas because he knows the people will need comfort and guidance when the memories come back to them. He wants to help them like he has helped Jonas.

3. The community will have to bear the memories because there is no one else to take them. The memories cannot go back to The Giver, and there is no one else ready to be trained as the next Receiver.

4. Jonas will not take the memories of music from The Giver because they are so special to him. When chosen as the Receiver of Memory, The Giver had the Capacity to Hear Beyond and Jonas wants him to have those memories after he has left.

Making Connections—Section 5:
Chapters 19–23 (page 62)

Student responses will vary. The choice of Sameness or Differences might need to be assigned to student groups in order to create a balanced debate.

Comprehension Assessment (pages 67–68)

1. B. eliminating differences in the community

2. E. "We relinquished sunshine and did away with differences."

3. Main Idea: The memories will return to the community.

4. B. The memories are growing weaker on Jonas's journey.; C. Jonas has trouble remembering snow.

5. H. People should make their own choices.

6. B. "I want to wake up in the morning and decide things!"

7. It is not good for just one person to hold all of the memories. Sharing the burden among many people is better for everyone.

8. G. "Jonas, you and I are the only ones who have feelings. We've been sharing them now for almost a year."